REBELLION

REBELLION

A MULTIMEDIA MEMOIR

By Amber Twyne

Disclaimer:
This book may contain subjects that are triggering such as child loss, abuse and alcoholism. Certain moments are exaggerated for emphasis.

DEDICATION

To my angel, Jade Star – such a short time but a lasting impact. Pumpkin, mommy will always love you.

To my Grandpa, James "Sonny" Crippen -- I miss you so much, "thanks a million"

To my Mommom, Mary "Spunky" Hopkins – I love and miss you and your contagious laugh.

Table of Contents

LETTER FROM THE AUTHOR

Hey Reader,

This book is probably like nothing you have ever read. There are quotes, poems, shorts, areas for your own thoughts, activities, just a bunch of stuff. I threw everything I learned about structure out of the window. I want you to really get a sense of my voice and understand me and where I'm coming from. I want this book to feel special to you, write in it, highlight, make notes, have at it! This is our journey, not just mine to walk alone. I've previously wasted a lot of time self-editing, so I went back and re-added after realizing no part of my story is "junk". This is not just about struggles. This is about rebelling against everything I thought I needed and should have had and instead learning to embrace the journey, rediscovering myself along the way.

Enjoy.

Love,
Amb

PREFACE

At twenty-six years old I found myself becoming complacent. I was comfortable with the concept of a pretty good middle-class way of living. I had a great job making good money for someone without a college degree but walking past pictures of concerts, seeing old mixtapes of the unsigned talent I used to manage and looking down at the promotional tee I designed for a street team I realized; I had given up on myself. I was getting caught up in a mundane routine that left me drifting farther and farther from the life I dreamed of as a child. I was so satisfied with being healthy and alive that I had forgotten what it was like to actually live.

I was haunted by my childhood dreams of being the next Oprah and each badge swipe into work confirmed that I was in a rat race for the next promotion in a career that I found comfortable, not ideal. I felt like I had lived the life of a 40-year-old woman before the age of 22. What was I thinking? How did I get to the point where a call center was what I deemed as a successful stopping point? Then I realized, I was so grateful to have survived situations that I thought only happened on Tyler Perry plays that I was just content with being a survivor.

INTRODUCTION

Let me start off by saying I've tried to write this book nine times. I don't mean nine drafts; I mean started over and was defeated nine times. In the words of my earthly idol, Erykah Badu, "I'm sensitive about my sh*t". With the covers of God Don't Like Ugly and I Know Why the Caged Bird Sings staring at me from the bookshelf across the room, I can feel an anxious twitch in my right eye. Comparing myself to the brilliant women before me, why would someone want to read a memoir about me? This is personal. I'm giving you a magnifying glass and asking you to zoom in and examine life through my eyes in a way that is far from conventional. Regardless, I'm committed. Even if it takes me ten, eleven or "fifty-leven" times of starting over. If my journey can help the next person, then it's worth it. My only ask is that if you find solace in this book, please share it with a friend.

WRITE THE BOOK

Go

#NowPlaying - Ready or Not by The Fugees

Yet again another sign.

How many times does God have to tell me to sit down and write this book?

I mean seriously, I ask for signs and confirmations, and when I get them, I ignore them like bad advice.

I make excuses for myself.

"Oh, I have time, Oprah didn't get her talk show until 45 and JK Rowling was cleaning houses in her 20s, I got time."

It is true, I may have time, but the urgency is not for me, it's for those young women out there NOW.

That need information NOW.

That are at the crossroads between a healthy and unhealthy situation RIGHT NOW!

I can't let any more time pass.

So here I go…..
I'm revving up…..
on my mark…..
get set…….
stop procrastinating……

and GO!

Make It Happen

WHAT'S ONE GOAL YOU REFUSE TO GIVE UP ON?

WHAT HAS BLOCKED YOU FROM ACHIEVING IT YET?

WHAT CAN YOU DO RIGHT NOW TO COMPLETE IT?

You Got This!

Internal Battle

#NowPlaying – Unholy War by Jacob Banks

There are internal battles going on.

I-have-a-story-to-tell
versus
must-I-relive-the-moments?

It-is-necessary
versus
It-hurts.

Who-will-read-this?
versus
what-if-just-one-life-is-changed?

The "what-if" wins.

DESIGN YOUR OWN BOOK COVER

WHAT WOULD YOUR TITLE BE? WOULD YOU USE AN ALIAS? WHAT COVER ART REPRESENTS YOUR STORY?

CHILDHOOD

A Thought
Childhood Environment

Kids are masterpieces created by every observation, it's not until you are an adult that you can appreciate teachings from your village, at that time deciphering the treasure from the junk. Children don't have the option to filter what knowledge sticks. They are at the whim of outside influence infiltrating their subconscious, shaping how they think and who they become.

COLORING
Page

Take a break and color me in!

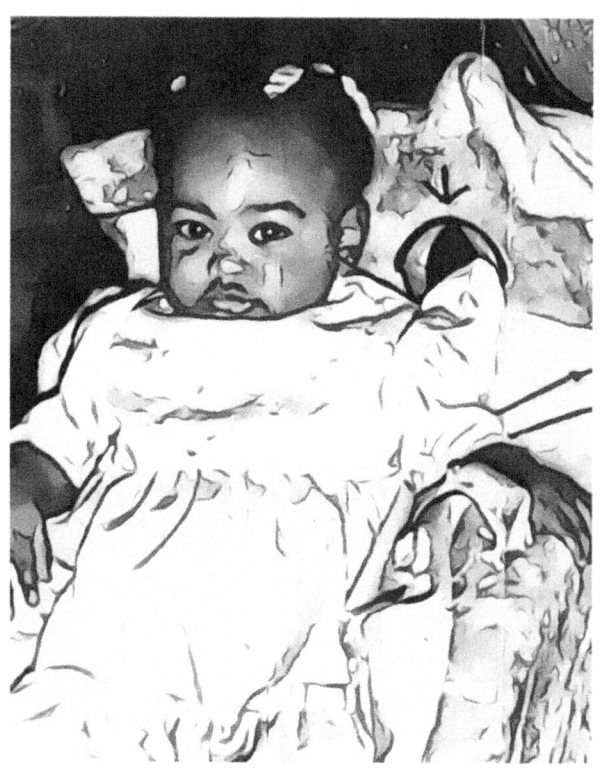

"It takes a village to raise an adult, but a child is a product of their environment."

FROM THE BEGINNING

It was the early 90s, two blocks down from our home church in West Philly. Running towards the aroma of homemade sweet potato pie in the air, "good morning" from grandma met with a warm hug and a taste of the batter. I hear the door, I take off running, dodging the fading animal statues strategically placed on both sides of the fish tank. Landing on the teal area rug that to me was a sea in the middle of the room, with the 3 tiers of house plants breaking up the sunrays from the balcony.

"Hey, hey!" peaking over the couch, straight from the barbershop, I know that high top fade down to the sneakers anywhere, it's the fresh prince, "hey Uncle Craig!"

Back down the hall, I hear my mom, following my trail first at the kitchen, then the fish, then the teal sea, I am her mini. Just as my mom and her little brother catchup, chatting about "what's going on" and laughing in sibling camaraderie, I hear the door again. I know those keys anywhere, "Grandpa's home!" announcing to the house as I run to meet him. Perfectly placing myself so the door couldn't hit me, but I'd be the first thing he sees.

"Hey sugie!" hit my ears as I squeeze him so tight! Careful not to knock down the bag that I know is a cheesesteak and chocolate milk meant just for me. Grandma is right behind me, never missing a chance to greet him with a kiss.

From the environment, to the social interactions, word choices and body language, I observed everything. This set the tone for how I believed a household should operate and how a family should be. The love infiltrated my subconscious, from martial longevity and affection down to the idea of multigenerational living. These circumstances laid the foundation for what I deemed as normal and aspired for my life to resemble.

MOM'S EASY SWEET POTATO PIE

INGREDIENTS

- 2 deep dish pie crusts
- 2 large cans of Bruce's Yams
- 1 cup brown sugar
- 1/2 cup white sugar
- 3 tsp lemon juice
- 1/4 tsp lemon extract
- 2 tsp cinnamon
- a splash molasses
- 1/2 tsp salt
- 1/2 tsp nutmeg
- 2 tsp vanilla extract
- 1/2 stick of butter
- 1/2 - 3/4 cup milk. Just enough to loosen batter
- 1 egg

DIRECTIONS

1. Combine ingredients except pie crust and egg in a large mixing bowl with potato masher and whip with fork. Taste test to your liking and once happy add egg and mix well.

2. Preheat oven to 350 degrees F

3. Pour mixture into pie crusts and bake in center of middle oven rack for 60-90 minutes or until desired color. Enjoy!

ONLY CHILD

Have you ever noticed an interaction between a single mom and her first child resembling best friends? As the first born, only child for four years, this was my reality. I was never put in daycare so the formative years of my development, when my mind was most vulnerable, I was my mom's travel buddy, attached to her hip and always on the move. When I wasn't with my mom, I was surrounded by adult family. In my eyes, I was equal and the concept of "stay in a child's place" was nonexistent. I can recall having full conversations, never being spoken to in gibberish, baby talk or incoherent slang. Concepts were never dumbed down to laymen's terms but actual conversations, that forced me, as a kid, to create my own opinions and form a way of critical thinking that was "above grade level". This was my normal and early on I was able to articulate myself properly and afforded a gift of trust, responsibility and independence. I loved it.

Our family is very close knit and for part of my young life, my mom and I lived with my grandparents, so I never had my own space. I needed to be able to get away and explore my thoughts and imagination. I started creating places where I would go lock myself in and enjoy the infinite space of my creativity. Cubby holes, closets, under the dining room table, inside the armoire, in the corner where the two couches met, anywhere I could call mine. My favorite of them all, the hallway closet that was almost packed to capacity. I shifted the contents around to make a personal cove with my treasures on each shelf. I would spend hours in there, participating in my favorite hobby, daydreaming.

FATHER

Throughout this chapter, you've heard me refer to different people in my family. My mom, my grandma, sisters, uncles – the squad. There is another important part of that squad that deserves his own story, my dad.

Just to clarify, I have a biological father and I have a dad, they are two very different people. You guys know the story. When a man and a woman love each other very much... (or maybe just thought they did, who can really know) – they partake in some adult activities, planned or unplanned, married or unmarried, birds and the bees, 9 months later and here I am. The happy ending in this case comes 2 years later, after divorce and my mom moving on, when Mr. Kevin comes into the picture. I don't remember my mom dating prior to that point. She never had me around strangers, I wasn't calling illegitimate men "uncle", I was shielded and protected from those types of situations and I knew full well who the other half of my genetics came from. When Mr. Kevin came around, I knew this was different. This guy wasn't like my uncles or my grandpa, even from that age I knew that his role in my life would be different than anything I had experienced already. My biological father had left early on, so I had no memory of quality time spent with him, this was all new to me.

My mom's relationship continued to grow, and one special valentine's day comes to mind. Every year my mom would buy me valentine's gifts, remember, we were attached at the hip. This year Mr. Kevin came over, brought gifts for my mom of course, but an extra something for me. It was a mini box of assorted chocolates and a valentine's day card with my favorite characters, the Muppet Babies! I loved it and kept it for years. Later after Mr. Kevin had left and me and my mom settled down for the night, I asked her "Can Mr. Kevin be my daddy?" "Are you sure? It's up to you." – yes, I was sure, and I began to cry. I had seen the dad and daughter relationship and never knew I wanted it. I didn't understand how it was missing. I didn't realize that I internalized the fact that I had a father that didn't seem to want me, but I have this man looking to step into that role. A few years later and we became a family, been tight ever since. So just to clarify, there is no stepdad or two half-sisters, that's my family. Period. Dad, thank you for stepping up!

One more thing that came with my dad was my mom mom. She loved me! Every visit felt like an opportunity to spoil me, like she was waiting on a grandchild and it was long overdue. God rest her soul. Thank you mom mom for taking me in as your own. For paying attention to me, learning my interests and treating me as an individual. Thank you for sharing your stories, your love and your laughs.

"GOOD HAIR"

Sitting by the kitchen stove in a chair pulled from the dining room. In one hand I have my rat-tail comb, in the other, a jar of Blue Magic hair grease. A brown tinged paper towel is eye level and smoke is in the air. For those that don't know, it's the night before Easter and my mom is hot combing my hair before church tomorrow.

"Your hair looks so nice straight and long," meant as a compliment, my grandma didn't know any better. As a dark-brown woman herself, with what we now call 4c hair, she had been told her whole life to fry, dye and lay those kinks to the side. So, from an early age, I associated straight hair with looking my best.

My mom has what our community would previously refer to as "that good hair", meaning not "nappy" tight coils, instead, she has thin, wavy hair, manageable with a wet brush. Clearly taking after my father's genetics, hot combs and box braids were the tools my tresses required. Wash days were the worst. My mom would need a break during the process, after the deep condition but right before the actual styling. Her break left me feeling exposed to the elements and embarrassment of anyone seeing this blown out, unruly lion's mane. I was self-conscious about how my natural hair looked and would begin to cry and hide to the sound of the doorbell, ducking behind the cushions to hide, for fear someone may see me looking ugly and unkempt.

The irony is I spent my adult years restoring that mane and she's a beauty, hear me roar!

PHILLY JAWN

"Where are you from?" Whenever I get that question, I have to pause for a second because it's asked with certain intent. If I say I'm from Philly, the response is, "you don't act like you're from Philly". If I say I'm from Delaware, that doesn't fully encompass what or who I am. So normally, my response is that I was born in Philly and raised in Delaware. The most accurate description of what environmentally shaped me, that's what people really want to know. What surroundings influenced how you think and what you preach?

West Philadelphia, born not raised. Inside the house, where I spent most of my days. We moved out of the city before I started kindergarten but continued to visit frequently for family. When I would go back to Philly as a kid and see my cousins, I felt like an outcast that wanted to fit in without the slightest clue as to what I wanted to fit into. Something as simple as going to the corner store was an adventure for me.

Anything they would say, I would absorb like a sponge, soaking up all the slang and expressive body language I could. I felt diluted by the suburbs and wanted to fill my cup with the colors of the city.

AWKWARD BLACK GIRL

A Thought
Childhood friendships

My very first friend group was made up of four girls; an African American, an Asian American, a European American and me. One, looking back, I'm impressed by the diversity of my school at that time and two, it is interesting to reflect on the ties that connect us. Our friendships were based on the simplest of things. Our favorite snacks, books to read and the colors of our backpacks. Our experiences were limited to only 5 years of life and we still had our childlike spark, not yet dimmed by the dark moments that, at times, comes with life's journey. At the time of writing this, unfortunately that friend group has long dispersed. One I remain connected with over social media, another moved away at a young age and I never heard from her again and one, sadly, passed away four years ago. That moment in time may have been easily forgotten but was precious and serves as a memory of innocent joy.

Whitney, Jamie & Timaree - my first friends, forever in my heart.

I love who I am

MY SPIRIT
SHINES BRIGHT

I AM A POSITIVE ROLE
MODEL FOR OTHERS

My ideas matter

**I make the
choice to be the
person I wish to
know**

I am strong –
physically,
mentally and
emotionally

I believe in my
dreams

I CHOOSE TO HAVE
A GREAT DAY

I inspire others with
my creativity

I WILL
NATURALLY
ATTRACT THE
VIBE I NEED
IN MY LIFE

ODYSSEY

Kindergarten was the first time I was around children that were strangers to me. I never attended daycare or preschool, so this opportunity to be around kids my own age and just interact was brand new. My first friends, a little black girl, a little Asian girl and a little white girl. I wasn't thinking about their heritage or the color of their skin. All I was thinking is "these girls are my age and we all like Lisa Frank stickers".

Fast forward a couple years and I'm in second grade. I took a test used to measure your comprehension and knowledge, in comparison to other students your age and grade level to determine how advanced you were, in relation to what the school board deemed was exemplary. I tested in the 97th percentile and with that came the opportunity to take part in Odyssey. Odyssey was the Academically Gifted Program for Advanced Youth. My counselor spoke to me and my mom about it and all I was thinking was how great it was going to be to have class with other kids that thought like me. The strategy was to send us, once a week, to another school with a classroom full of kids from the other schools in the district to attend these Odyssey classes. It was described with the best selling techniques in the book.

There were four kids from my school, grades ranging from first through third grade. Surprised by how few students were participating from my school and even more so by the fact that I was the only black girl. How, in a school with a student body over six hundred kids, was one of four and the only black girl? I couldn't wrap my head around it.

When we finally arrived at the new school, me and the girl in my grade, get to the classroom to see there are kids from the other schools, about sixteen students total. Yet, and still, I was the only black girl. Feeling like the literal, black sheep, academically I knew I was supposed to be here. I tested in, that was my proof, but between their vocabulary and the camaraderie they were building between each other based on their geographic locations and societal similarities, I felt like an alien.

Going from classes where diversity is a strength, to this environment that looks like an ad for Aeropostale, I was out of my element. The only thing we had in common was our ability to score high on a test.

Reflection
Mrs. H

I'm convinced that my fifth-grade teacher was a racist. Here are some examples of how I felt targeted or completely ignored in her class.

One of our vocabulary words was "niggardley".
nig·gard·ly
/ˈnigərdlē/
adjective
not generous; stingy.
"serving out the rations with a niggardly hand"

She debated with me in front of the class, loud and wrong, about the difference between rubbing alcohol and peroxide. Stating alcohol is for an open wound, foams up and doesn't burn and peroxide is used for muscle aches and burns if over open flesh. I repeated multiple times that was the exact opposite, even stating peroxide is in the brown bottle and alcohol in the clear, but to no avail.

Another public classroom debate with me, when I answered sodium chloride is table salt and she told me I was wrong, it's poisonous and that sodium chloride is rock salt used to de-ice the streets (FYI, that's calcium chloride, again, she was loud and wrong.)

The last and most memorable was the family tree project. She had us trace our family trees back to the original countries of origin. You already know where this is going. The farthest I could go back to at that time (pre-ancestry DNA test) was South Carolina and at the end of my presentation she told me, in front of the class, that I didn't do enough research.

Needless to say, my children will be homeschooled and I'm glad she retired. What a witch.

A Thought

Segregation

In my early drafts of this book, I went into detail about my school experience. One aspect of that was the detrimental nature of segregating students based on academics. I can understand, from a practical perspective, how students studying the same subjects would generally be in the same classes and such, but in my middle school, the higher ups thought it was a good idea to designate an entire hallway.

Now I'm not an expert in adolescent psychology, but it doesn't take a genius to see how separating students based on their curriculum and condemning them to specific hallways would be an issue. Division and communal complications that can, and in my case DID, negatively impact the social development and community of the student body. Everyone noticed the modern-day segregation. The elitist mentality that it created was problematic, had these suburban white kids thinking they were above everyone else. It caused insecurities in the minorities stuck in hallways with those students, feeling isolated from their distant peers. Not to mention bullying that resulted from the outright disconnect of the situation.

That choice had such a deep impact that it found its way in my book. Two words - do better.

IN A BLACK GIRL BODY

Junior year in high school is where I first developed my social identity. Prior to, I had gone through years of being teased and isolated by other black kids since second grade and I didn't know how to interact naturally. How do I start the process of building a network of people that looked like me? Being in academically gifted classes, as they were called, I was often thrown in a category with white people as if I was the one of a kind, token black, or the black girl in rare form. That created a sense of "oh you're a white girl trapped in a black girl's body", often called "Oreo" and other subconsciously damaging terms, as if my skin was a prison to who I was inside. I can recall embracing this self-hate speech at one point, not realizing the poisonous veins of white supremacy had pervaded my way of thinking.

"The paradox of education is precisely this - that as one begins to become conscious one begins to examine the society in which he is being educated." - James Baldwin

As a melanated person in American society, we are assimilating with the people that oppress us. It is a constant effort to take off the distorted lenses put on our eyes against our will. In my adulthood, I still find myself struggling to juggle my implicit bias, unlearning to re-learn and other societal balls of confusion in an attempt to "wake-up".

Surrounded by students, that didn't look like me. Facing microaggressions from teachers that see one black student in a class of eighteen and believe that's an accurate representation of academic honors in our community. Being taught from a curriculum that excelled in whitewashing history, meant to disempower and erase us. These external influences 5 days a week, are toxic to a child that hasn't even fully developed social skills yet and in my youthful ignorance, I accepted their perception of black children like me.

What Do You See

#NowPlaying – I Am Not My Hair by India Arie

What do you see when you look at me?

Do you see a short black girl with boobs, small frame, piercings and tatts?

Or do you see a young African American woman with the curvature of her ancestors, adorned in her modern-day version of tribal art? Sporting a glare representing the fire that fuels her self-motivation.

What do you hear?

Do you hear a high-pitched voice piercing across the room?

Or do you hear my emotions, my vulnerability and the aggression desperately fighting to be heard by any means necessary, despite each insecurity and self-conscious thought that tries to force my silence?

What do you taste?

Do you taste my cherry flavored Chapstick, with hints of winter mint, tingling the buds on your tongue?

Or do you taste the passion in my pucker, my lust for who I hope that you are, holding my breath, not to get my hopes up too far for fear of disappointment?

What do you smell?

Is it the floral vanilla accented fragrance midst against my skin's natural essence?

Or is it my Egyptian musk covered blood, sweat and tears seeping through my skin, constantly shed in a mad man's attempt to make my aspirations a successful reality?

What do you feel?

Do you feel the cold touch of my fingertips and the scratch of my manicured nails against your skin?

Or do you feel the callouses of a hard worker, scratching and clawing through the rat-race, working myself to the bone?

What do you feel?

Are your senses creating the accurate picture?

Or must you search deeper than that physical,

To truly see, hear, taste, smell or touch me?

Awkward Black Girl

#NowPlaying – Window Seat by Erykah Badu

I was just a girl. Trying to figure out who I was and where I fit in. There didn't seem to be many places that matched my interests.

Just an "awkward black girl" as far as THEY were concerned.

Had my nose in some book, talking about the "fun facts" that I had whizzing around my brain.

My vocabulary was missing the cussing and was instead influenced by my "word of the day".

I didn't watch 106 & Park, instead I was watching *That's So Raven* re-runs and singing along with *The Cheetah Girls*.

My glasses and box braids with the baby hairs gelled down, a true 90s baby.

Gen pop couldn't appreciate it.

I had just started high school and already I was over it, ready for my ticket out.

AWKWARD OR AN ORIGINAL?

TIME TO HIGHLIGHT SOME STRENGTHS

What are some of the character traits that you've been criticized about? What others or yourself see as character flaws?

Now acknowledge why all those traits can be strengths! How can they be used for good and positive intentions?

37

Who Do You Think You Are?

#NowPlaying – Ghetto Supastar by Pras ft ODB & Mya

I am an artist.

I utilize various aspects of media to portray an image of me.

Amber Twyne,
Queen Kareem,
Miss Serene Melodie.

The sides of me that most often don't see.

And for those who do,
I must genuinely care
and have great love for thee
because, you see,
offering
this side of me is
everything
but easy.

A constant battle,
trying to get others to respect me,
being bossy when I'm actually needy.

Pushing away when I want to be clingy.

Repressing the emotions
and forcing that voice to whisper to itself
silently.

All done with grace poetically.

I am an artist.

LOVE AND WAR

Let's Talk

#NowPlaying – Can We Talk by Tevin Campbell

Can we talk for a minute boo?
There's a couple things I gotta say.
Can I really be real with you?
Before obstacles get in our way.
Before outsiders cause confusion,
While problems cease to exist,
Before time together becomes mundane,
While I'm still thinking of our kiss...
Our moments, my emotions replaying in my head.
Feelings develop but lust is only a factor in my bed.
Your conversation, truly, is what feeds my mind.
I find you so intriguing, though, I've known you for a short time.
When put into perspective, I've only known you for a minute.
So, hear me out, loud and clear, before the excitement reaches its limit.
Before you start to grow weary of texts on break or late-night calls.
Before you find yourself no longer tolerant of my flaws.
Let's talk about those moments when I pause before I speak.
Let me voice that silence, when I look away as our eyes meet.
If you promise not to judge me,
I hope you don't misconstrue,
It's not that I'm "thirsty",
I'm just really attracted to you...

A Thought

Learning about love

How do we learn about relationships? Realistically how many of us have gotten a sit-down with our parents, guardians, loved ones, et cetera and just talked about love? I'm not talking about God's love. If you grew up in a Christian household, I am sure you have heard all about God's love and can recite John 3:16 by heart. I'm not talking about an only begotten son here; I'm talking about the love we interact with on this earthly plane. Everything I learned about relationships was based on what I saw from the outside looking in with my immature eyes. It wasn't until my mid-twenties did, I realize fairy tale love was not a realistic nor healthy love goal. Don't get me wrong, there is no blame to be placed on the adults in my life, many of us are still trying to figure out what we want ours to look like. There is no cookie cutter, paper doll-life that breaks the mold for everyone. Even those relationships that I admired from the outside had their fair share of compromise that I may or may not wish to emulate. With that in mind, where do you begin? Where is the balance between celebrating the fun of finding a special connection and still reinforcing discipline and imposing healthy boundaries? If you make it sound too great you pose the risk of your hormonal teen trying to fulfill this fantasy. If you are too strict, you just might find a rebel on your hands, especially if your child starts to get taught by his/her peers.

Indescribable Feelings Described

#NowPlaying – Hate How Much I Love You by Neyo

Love of
my life, heart for my soul, sanity for my mind.
Our love is truly one of a kind.
Misunderstood by many,
very few can relate
nor simulate
the extent of a bond so great.
Grand - superb - magnifique,
overwhelmingly unbelievable,
I can barely speak.
Thoughts in a whirlpool of emotions that
overpower,
divide and conquer
the essence of logical thinking
that my brain naturally follows.
But why?
Why can't I put the pieces
of this puzzle in order according to sequence?
Instead I throw them in ecstasy,
creating a masterpiece accidently.
Serenity
in its craziest form.
Ain't neva felt nothin like this before.
No longer am I torn
because the only thing I fear and mourn
is … the loss of love.
Mmm … Love.
A concept
so complex
yet a feeling so simple.
A gift.
God decided to share a piece of heaven
or better yet a piece of Himself.

More valuable than the world's wealth.
Love.

Life.
Optimism.
Victory.
Ecstasy.

With this, I don't need no drugs, I'm on a natural high.
Get back Satan, victory is mine.
Pessimism has no place in me, with this life,

Filled with love,

I can breathe easy.

#NowPlaying – What Is Love by V Bozeman

I had no business there.
In the mental space where I thought,
That I occupied the emotional maturity,
To physically say,
"I love you".

A Thought

Gaslighting

By definition, gaslighting is the process of someone using psychological techniques to manipulate others. In abusive relationships, this is commonplace and a key factor in the victim feeling unable to leave. Recognize the signs. The abusers may lie, deny facts and mix lies with truth, causing confusion and make it hard to know what's reality. They may mix insults and compliments, hurting your self-esteem only to praise you for their own benefit. Not enough to give you confidence, just enough for security. They may fill you will false hope by saying all the right things, but actions reflect nothing. Finally, they will pull you away from your support system and turn others against you, while making themselves look like the person you need. This is not exclusive to masterminds, the common abuser uses these techniques, trust me, I've experience it firsthand and it can happen to anyone.

If you are in a dangerous or abusive (physical, mental and/or emotional) relationship call the National Domestic Violence Hotline for help 1-800-799-7233,

1-800-787-3224 for TTY, or if you're unable to speak safely, you can log onto thehotline.org or text LOVEIS to 22522.

"BOYFRIEND"

I didn't have my first "boyfriend" until I was in 11th grade, which to be honest, at that time, I didn't even know what a boyfriend was. I just wanted to be able to say that I had one and make some sort of "Saved by the Bell" TV fantasy my reality. You know, walk my books to class, be my date to the dance, important high school stuff.

Prior to, I had lied and made up guys just so I wouldn't feel like an oddball. "Oh yeah, my boyfriend is great too, his name is Dante, he doesn't go here, he's from Philly and my cousin introduced us" the lies I told. Peer pressure had gotten the best of me, pathetic. When the opportunity presented itself to actually have a real person to claim, I was here for it. After a couple dances, rides home from school, a date or two and an innocent kiss here or there, we broke up. I don't even remember why or what happened and to be honest I don't even consider the experience to count as a relationship outside of the purposes for this book.

The reason why it was important is because I need you to know exactly how young-minded I was. In 11th grade, I was socially equivalent to maybe today's 6th grader. I was a child who didn't know what a "French kiss" was. I still looked away at kissing scenes in the movies for goodness sakes. I was not prepared for a relationship. I wish I knew it was okay to be a kid.

"I'm hesitant in writing this portion. Like the threat of Beetlejuice, say his name three times and he appears."

Reflection
The Relationship

I thought I could do it, but it's too much. I've shared my side of the story verbally so many times but for some reason to write it down on paper and see it in words is overwhelming. This is the section of the book that has held me up the longest. That has got me re-thinking, re-writing, deleting suppressing, all of the above. However, that's the beauty of a true partner in love. They are strong in the ways you need support. So, I'll have my true soul mate, share this part of my story. Thank you sweety.

Thoughts B4 Bed

#NowPlaying – Lost in Love by Skillz (Quan Kareem)

For you deserve more than a temporary fix
more than a blind fold over your heart
and cheap parlor tricks

That isn't love or magic
it's wrong and disastrous
it ain't even autumn
an' you fallin'
for a man who won't catch you when clearly you need to leave!

Let that marinade
so it can simmer into your mental,
that you deserve better

And for every left turn you make,
he comes right and does you wrong
and then comes crying bac wit a love letter?

Till his hand raises,
and the bottles empty
then you'll be screaming
get off of me

Next time what if nobody is around to call the police
Hello-
Check ya side kick
cuz that bruise shoulda been left on those side chicks
Man look what pride gets
Better yet look what Twyne gets!

Longing for a fairy tale kiss
will have you sleeping wit a fish,
how can you stand it?

Ok ok ok, maybe I'm being too hard,
maybe I don't understand,
maybe this ain't none of my business
and it's all part of ya plan

Sigh.... Female logic
anyway next topic
I promised I would always be there
For support, long or short,
the terms would be fair
You would hit me wit adventure just to let down ya hair
Have it blowing in the wind, singing oldies in Bear

Sam cooking wit Tammy
half a bottle wit Tonya
I only brought you around family,
cuz your well worth the honor

Remember back in the days, chilling wit Dj and Ana
Now we up every night tryna make us a lil lasagna
But I can see it inside ya
Amber Twyne was meant for designer,
not all that BS and drama

Crazy, sexy, and cool
all that and some chips
I mean I'm staring at ya pic,
sitting here, thinking bout them lips,
and ya long gentle kiss

Sh*t if I close my eyes and sniff..
I can still smell ya fragrance in a deep erotic abyss
Dark liquor on my tongue from that bottle of whisk,
but I still feel bad cuz you had to hide that shit
When just the other night we was hot 96

You got sum baggage
But I think i'm loving the trips

Flaws and all, I be inhaling ya pifs
Because It's 1:41 and I'm missing you

I wrote a poem instead of that rhythm and blues
reminiscing bout those days with the Rugrats cartoon,
or how bout that ocean no sharks or harpoons
Haha yea I'm talking bout you

And how you swoon me like you do
Now it might not be our time but your only thirsty if u want
more juice!

You deserve: a night under the stars
You deserve: no pain and no scars

You deserve: something slight, like your dreams
You deserve: a little trust and honesty
You deserve: a man that knows how you feel
And the only way to see it, is to let your heart heal

I'm saying Cupid is stupid if he keeps shooting so ruthless..
I mean It takes time and precision to end up wit the right
decision
So don't rush your thoughts, stop ignoring your heart, and
make that man understand that you can do better apart!

Refreshed or oppressed…how do you wish to wake up?
Bruised, battered, blood splattered in the tub
Or Singing opera, dancing ratchet and applying make-up? Lol
Yea I took it to the extreme, but how many chances will u
gamble your body. The temple that is god's creation wasn't
made for a slow demise.

VENT SESSION

Most of us have a love story, either one of heartbreak or one of triumph. A fantasy or a nightmare. Share yours, whether it's fictional or truth.

Speech Is Golden

#NowPlaying – Respect by Aretha Franklin

Every sentence, every line, every word, every syllable.

Each sound from my lips is shut down in an attempt to stifle me.

Why me?

I see how my femininity conflicts with the male discussion, that could be it.

Perhaps my tone of voice is too much for your ears to bear?

Or is it..... me?

Is my presence now irksome to you?

Oh, I see.

All the time is too much, none of the time is too little, and some of the time is perfect when it's under your agenda.

Hope you enjoyed it and heeded my words because silence is now the treatment and you'll soon learn....

SPEECH IS GOLDEN.

Breaking Point

#NowPlaying – Man Down by Rihanna

Patience is wearing thin
My tense brow and stern lips
Balled fists, I can't sit
I'm bout to snap.
I'm beat up, I'm torn down
My chest hurts, a scorned scowl
Blood pressure is high now
I'm bout to snap.
My eyes bawl, I'm not sad
The tears fall, getting mad
Frustration strong, reactions bad
I'm bout to snap.
You test me, I warned you
You tried me, you swore too
I'm trying to ignore you
But I'm bout to snap.
It's building up, you wore me out
This is what I be talking bout
All this stress, I could do without
I'm bout to snap.
You point the blame, you do me wrong
You tell me lies, the same old song
Second guessing if I'm strong
Cuz I'm bout to snap.
It's getting bad, I'm at my peak
No more lies, no more deceit
Such a tangled web we've weaved
I'm bout to snap.

And then.... into a million different pieces, all the pain resulting in an outpour of unfiltered, organic, authentic, unadulterated, inevitable emotional breaking point pieces.... In the form of wet cries, deep sighs and tabloid headlines read...."She Snapped".

List the people you KNOW
love and care about you
and your BEST INTEREST!

My Support
System

MOTHERHOOD

Pay It Forward

SHARE SOME ADVICE FOR THE
FUTURE GENERATION

I Answered

#NowPlaying – Far Away by Marsha Ambrosius

I answered your call because she was with you.
She was with you because you previously called the police.
The police told me I would be kidnapping if I took her with me.
With me is where she belonged, my first born.
"My first born, I'm her mother!" my words echoed in the courthouse.
In the courthouse, my custody paperwork, it is still processing.
It is still processing, riding behind the ambulance.
The ambulance took her to the emergency room.
The emergency room is where I watched them try to save her.
Save her, I just wanted to save her, but it was so sudden.
Sudden Infant Death Syndrome, that's what they called it.
Called it unexplained, couldn't tell me what happened.
What happened that I got to this point?
This point in my life where everything I had envisioned took a drastic turn.
Turn the page to my testimony, got my call.
My call, on a mission for women, I answered.

My Angel

#NowPlaying – Zion by Lauryn Hill

While you were inside of me,
sharing my same heartbeat,
being my companion constantly,
I would sing,
"Angel".

I didn't know that would be the case literally.
And to be honest I feel guilty.
I anticipated an eternity & now I only have you spiritually
for infinity.

I look for you in random ways and places,
on different faces
and sometimes I start spacing
and my heart starts racing because,

I
can
see
you....

But back to reality,
people would think I'm crazy,
but they don't understand....
You are my baby.

The reason why I know what happiness is.
And I will be your living legacy.

........I love you pumpkin.

WORD SEARCH

```
P N S F F Q F X W Q V W E K L U R Z O J Z Z Y U G W R J T I
J Y R O Y V E V V H M D U M O F X P K X N V L E G A C Y Y Z
E V C D K V F P C B T F H Z W O M E N F L Y U T Q V Q D Y H
P K Y F K D A X U A B Z F N Z S Z N G Y W O Z Q G Z H G S R
V O K K E C Q B U U I T J B M R R Y G P H E M H Q J X K H G
N C H E M A X A H G T M N U E A I S G I B C U G S D B C G Q
U U P D V T F U V D H K O J I A T W W W M H C U W P J P A B
Y G J B L L K L S E W X P M F D U J W G O I T R W U N A T W
M V G P X N J K Q K O Y L S E P F T Z R T L N N E M Q T P J
K P C D C D Y V F B J H U M G W X P Y Z H D U L G P G Z S V
N M O M M A L H G Z G T G I H Q S J O W E C B X B K E H I V
R A A U L V I T A Q Z D O S M C V B O H R P Y V N I G C H S
O X C U O P A R U X E I Q C Q L O I H H E U R A D N N F A O
V G V B V C C K E M N K D W Q H B J A R Q A P E P O P O N K
J E E S N A A L G I P M J U K I Y M C C K T R V G S V O A W
S F B B G G N L K B G Q Q N F T T W S H P R S T Y N G H L F
Y X S X M J G O F S J N M G F H V F X K Z B D A B F A D A M
L Y L Q E E E V G K P P M I Z W G T T G A L N Q M E K N R I
U Q Q M N F L E T X E I R W V U E K B V Z O Z V M R A N C L
M K I E I W G I C K I T P Y E U C X L X B S T S E Z J T F Y
P D L Y C S G Y N N C L E O F J T P Q L Z W H L Z Q Y C Z Q
B I X E H B S L G A Q M Q R D K Y I O H H E N R H I D O E W
J C Q U D B D I O H C S N Q N F G F K D C E B F Q Q U M O R
Y M O M M Y Y V O W V F Q K J I B Q U P N T M A Q B U J R M
E M V E G M S R V N N Q C E Y O T Q W E J Y W K B V F I T Y
C N O G V J D A U G H T E R V R W Y F K I A J V A Y O V E U
J N I V T D K N P G A P M I W T L H A D V K D G S M Y S W G
W D D I V L Q Q O X T C I B E L L Y W B P G P E Z H B C M P
D V X V D H G S I N G D K U W K E M W E H D S W D C Y E E A
F H L S M E R L E D Q F Q J O C J O I W E F X L O C S V R G
```

heartbeat	pregnancy	eternity	daughter
pumpkin	mission	legacy	sweety
mother	melina	beauty	reign
belly	women	angel	mommy
momma	amber	child	love
baby	jade	glow	sing
mom			

REBEL

Life is a

MAZE

The journey isn't always easy. There are twists, turns, even some dead ends. Sometimes we have to go back and re-walk a path we've already traveled in order to reach the finish line.

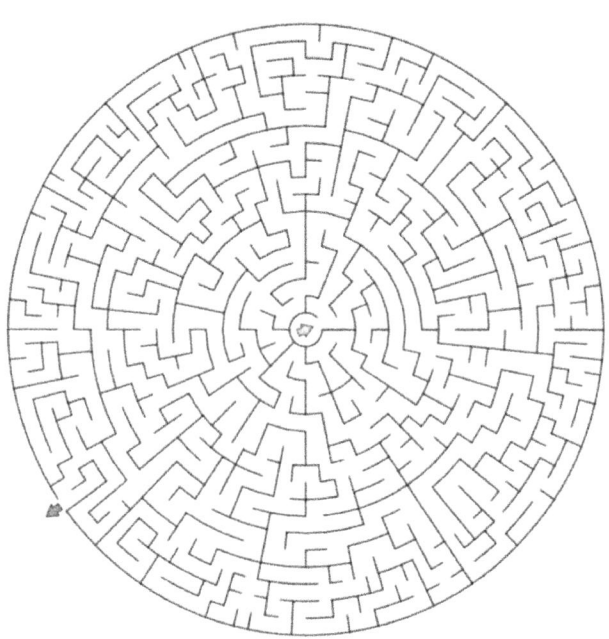

Black Mirror
#NowPlaying - Girl on Fire by Alicia Keys

What happened to the girl?

She's a bold woman with a fire and desire that Rick & Teena couldn't match.

She's on the dark side of the mirror.

Same eyes but with a stronger passion.

A yearning daredevil who was waiting to break free.

She went from holding her tongue to speaking words strong enough to break you.

Who is this girl?

A Thought
Rebellion

In psychology, rebellious behavior is understood to be an indicator of a need to deviate from societal norms in an attempt at liberating oneself from a situation. I was overwhelmed from trying to be put into boxes my whole life and then I couldn't take it anymore. I ran from any and everything that bear the slightest resemblance to what was familiar. That drastic change was reckless and full of mistakes, however, out of that phase I learned and remembered who I am, and I will never forget it again.

PARTY GIRL

I was never a party girl. I wasn't ever the person invited or known for hosting them. I was an awkward little black girl. Even in high school when I started attending dances, I would show up in something I put together, never the trendiest, but it was me. I would dance and allow the music to flow through my limbs channeling my ancestral rhythm. I appreciated the opportunity to be myself and be free. On the dance floor was the only place I was safe from being teased. Here, I wasn't an outcast subjected to ridicule. Almost like I embodied a different person, so I named her - De'avian Mahogany, Miss D.

A mix between Tracy "Mahogany" Chambers played by Diana Ross and "De'avian" from Sister Sister and every character actress Alexis Fields was type-casted into, Miss D represented living freely while speaking my truth unapologetically.

Miss D was an excuse. She was something I could blame my rebellion on. A character that I could dress up and give a script to. A character that could verbalize what I was feeling.

I was in control, like a screenplay writer develops her protagonist, I could manipulate her to get my point across. Miss D was my puppet. Every time I went out, it was a chance for me to use her to put on a show. She gave me permission to show off and show out.

ANOTHER SHOT

I stared into the eyes of a reflection I didn't recognize. I stood in the bathroom of college dorm, smeared mascara and matted burgundy weave, reeking of cheap vodka and cough syrup. The last thing I remember is belting out lines of Crew Love, not realizing that I fit those lyrics so perfectly. How did I get here?

Not here as in apartment B on Campus road—but here; a place in my mind where sex, drugs and clubs were common, and my alter ego does all the thinking for me. Her name is Miss D. She flows so perfectly, a disguise to hide the person I had smothered and cast away. I made the conscious decision to live in a state of emotional unconsciousness and let her take over.

At this rock bottom, I lived like I didn't care if I would see tomorrow. Reckless, hasty, and nonchalant about morality and shame. Daily escapades of "finding the next move" was a way for me to stay in a state of constant distraction. I'd gotten to the point where I couldn't stand to be alone because the disgust, I felt from my own actions hurt me more than the hangovers.

Self-medication with a daily dose of Bacardi and an injection of "insert friend here" was the treatment of choice. I noticed the type of people that began gravitating toward me had the same disregard for themselves and urge to live for any form of attention. Where did all my friends go? Why was I surrounded with "turn up queens"? If birds of a feather fly in the same flock, then what did that make me? And who was I to judge? Too many questions I had to ask myself. Thankfully, my medication helped me to avoid facing the answers. Miss D wasn't any better than them, but I knew Amber was.

I cried for her to come to and break out of the comatose that I inflicted. I hoped that maybe the tears would purge the past eight months out of my system. Maybe if I got in the shower long enough, I could wash away all my sins. If I move far away to where nobody knows me, I could start over. There's banging on the door. "Hurry up before I throw up on the floor!" I could hear my friend shuffle around the hall outside. Drunk and lost. A fellow flock member. And with that, I remembered that I'm still in front of the mirror in a random apartment with my eyes bloodshot from crying and too much drinking. I want another shot.

THE "FUN DRUNK"

Free alcohol from suckers helped me to subdue my personal pain at their expense. "Can I buy you a drink?" turned out to be my favorite pick up line.

Soon enough, I discovered it was a loaded question and a not so innocent gesture. It came with expectations, but I had just gotten my "all access pass" being a few days over twenty-one and I wasn't hip to the tricks of the opposite sex. I'm not saying that every guy who bought me a drink ended up getting my number but the idea of a man believing that he could redeem a prize for a rum and coke was a concept that I found to be brand new.

"Oh yeah," they would say while rubbing their chin. "I remember you from that party last week." Or I might hear, "Wasn't it you with that light skinned girl at that kickback last Saturday?" My reputation preceded me, and not in the way that I had hoped. I was even getting messages in my inbox, bargaining complimentary club entry in exchange for sharing the event on social media. Who could turn down hanging out with the turn up queen? Talk about a social media socialite! As a young woman, I was working odd jobs so I wasn't bound by a strict schedule that would devoid me of turn up time. Even without a car, finding a ride to the party was never a problem because being Miss D had its perks. The more parties I went to, the more people I mingled with, the better the invites became. Eventually I started arriving to clubs and being escorted straight to VIP, with no cost for cover, drinks, or transportation. I went from city to city and living on my own meant nobody to monitor my whereabouts at any given moment. I'd watched enough Law and Order to know how dangerous that is, but that didn't stop me. I was never really into drugs, to me, watching David Ruffin get high in The Temptations left enough of a bad taste in my mouth, as far as drugs were concerned. Even my grandpa smoking a pack of cigarettes a day made me not want to go anywhere near cigarettes. Alcohol was my drug of choice. It was always glorified in the media and that made it more acceptable to me. With such easy access to it, there was no reason for me not to indulge. My mom always feared for me drinking alcohol. My dad was an alcoholic and the idea that alcoholism could possibly be hereditary always left her wide-eyed when I had anything more than a half-glass of wine. No matter how many hangovers, black outs, or embarrassing drunken stories I could never refuse. I was the "fun drunk" that kept the party rolling, got the people coming, down for whatever.

EXIT, STAGE LEFT

On one particular night, I made plans to have a girls' night out at a popular beach bar. I had just installed some auburn Badu-inspired braids that fell down my back to my mid-thigh and perfectly highlighted my skin tone with a hint of golden red strands. Looking slim-thick, I was rocking multi-colored print tights from my local hood store, that accentuated my newly developed curves and the remnants of my child-bearing assets. A red tank top followed the fullness of my breasts and nobody could tell me nothing. From the moment I stepped out of the car, my rhythmic walk commanded the attention of anyone I passed. Bypassing the line outside didn't help my already unhealthy ego and I strut right to the center of the dance floor, without hesitation nor shame.

I felt the DJ catching my vibes because he was playing nothing but hits that resonated with me. From classic hip hop tracks, to a Beyoncé mix, then finally Reggae, my jam. I was slow winding as if I was putting on a personal show for someone special. Taking breaks only to hit the bar, where men were waiting to see what I was drinking and if they could refill my glass. I had businessmen approach me, talking about corporate cards and hotel rooms, "in case I needed a place to stay for the night". I had college kids too scared to approach me, getting pep talks and coaxing from their friends, to step forward. Then, mid dutty-wine, the DJ called me to the stage. Amber was too shy to take the bait, but Miss D, full of liquid courage, stormed the stage and put on a show.

The way she was twerking, working and jerking you would think I was getting paid to entertain the crowd. When I turned around and saw all the phones out and cameras flashing on me I realized this is not the attention I wanted. This is not how I wanted other people to perceive me. The proverbial Miss D was laughing at me now from the wing of the stage, popcorn and cocktail in hand, and I was stuck with this one woman show. I snatched the keys out of my friend's hand and stormed out of the club to the car. I could hear the stagger of their unsteady heels behind me.

Now, fully sober, I threw my heels in the backseat and rushed my friends to get in the car, so I could speed away as fast as possible from this situation. The icing on the cake was an arrogantly thirsty man, I looked up to see, leaning in my car window.

"Miss, can I come with you?"

"No and get off my door!" I spat, in complete disbelief that he had the audacity to think I was this approachable. I'm a good girl. An honor student. Miss D made his perception of me all wrong.

"You were the one on stage, right?"

He spat back, pulling away just a bit to get a good look at me. He was right. I was the one on stage. I was the one that showed up dressed specifically for eyes to reach my untouchables. I was the one that danced, reenacting the very action he thought he was getting tonight. Finally, my friends had found their way to the car. "She's not interested, sorry," my homegirl offered her drunken explanation in slurred words. He finally got the hint to back off. I took my version of the walk of shame, out of the driver seat to the passenger and cried with my head pressed against the window. The lustful intentions of an inebriated audience left me feeling filthy and covered in sweat. All I wanted was a bath and to undo everything I had just done.

DRUNKEN THOUGHTS

During my rebellious stage, I grew a dependency for the limelight. When dancing to my own beat was no longer enough to make me the center of attention, I pushed past my own limits and became somebody I didn't recognize. Even Miss D was shocked to see how I had lost all control.

Drunk again, in my apartment this time, all alone. Sulking in the bathtub listening to Marsha Ambrosius' album on repeat wishing I was far, far away. Crying, drinking wine that I stole from a party earlier that week because I knew I would need a fix later and didn't have money to buy it. The alcohol was making me hungry but the only thing in my fridge was half-eaten contents in a McDonald's bags from the night before. I didn't have enough money to go grocery shopping and three dollars spent on the dollar menu was in my budget. The panic of trying to escape my situation kept me from thinking long enough to react to it in a way that made sense. I was in a state of reacting to everything that I felt happened to me. Being depressed, domestic abuse, racism, pressure of perfection, teenage pregnancy, infant child loss, depression, anxiety, criticism, crushed dreams and guilt. I felt it was too much to deal with, so I was letting Miss D handle the situations that I wanted nothing more to do with. I wanted to live life with no attachments. Twenty-one years of living like a square peg trying to fit in a circle would have you living fast and hard, too.

When you are so anti-self and you don't care what happens, you'll do anything fearlessly.

Still suspended in the now cold water in this tub, daydreaming about what my life could have been.

DEATH OF MISS D

I was tired. That was it. I realized I was tired of this lifestyle, but running away wasn't an option. I knew I had to get rid of her, in order to live a life worth salvaging. I had to sacrifice Miss D to save myself. It's hard to give up and disconnect yourself from someone that you depended on as your support system for so long. Someone that built your confidence and encouraged you in moments of uncertainty. Just like every toxic relationship, you have to know when to leave and put yourself first. You have to realize when the negative influence of someone else is hindering your progress, your safety and putting your life at risk. That's what she was now to me, toxic. The confidence was no longer a positive characteristic trait. It had grown into a cockiness that blurred my vision. I began veering off the straight and narrow path. The twists and turns took me deeper and deeper into this maze until I found myself backed into a corner. In that moment, when your survival instincts are kicking in, I understood it was either her or me. I chose me and she had to go.

Cutting ties had to be quick, succinct and ruthless, clearing any residual remnants of her influence. No wild girls' night out nor a short trip to Philly. I dropped it cold turkey, like the bad habit it was. While backed into this corner I reversed the roles and stifled her voice. Taking revenge on those times that I was speaking outside of my character and vocalizing wants that didn't reflect my inward desires. All the times when seductive remarks dripped from her lips, I made her eat her words. For every glance at the wrong guy, I blinded her with my recollection of the goals where I need to keep my sights. I bound up her body for each inch of excessive skin she revealed on my behalf. I subdued her into the sunken place for which I had risen, so that she could view the life I was meant for while being paralyzed as a surreal nightmare of my subconscious.

The final step was stabbing her in the black hole where her heart should've been with the knifes from the backs of friends I'd abandoned.

There she was laying on the cold ground of my past. With a tombstone over her grave,

"Here lies Miss D, a constant reminder of the skeletons I buried of bad nights past."

Bad Habit Brainstorm

Nobody is perfect, what are some habits and behaviors you need to break. Write them out and work on them! No better time like the present.

HEALING

SELF-CARE SCHEDULE

TASKS	M	T	W	T	F	S
_____	☐	☐	☐	☐	☐	☐
_____	☐	☐	☐	☐	☐	☐
_____	☐	☐	☐	☐	☐	☐
_____	☐	☐	☐	☐	☐	☐
_____	☐	☐	☐	☐	☐	☐
_____	☐	☐	☐	☐	☐	☐
_____	☐	☐	☐	☐	☐	☐
_____	☐	☐	☐	☐	☐	☐

INCORPORATE SOME
ACTIVITIES FOR YOUR SELF
CARE INTO YOUR ROUTINE.
PRAYER, MEDITATION,
EXERCISE, WRITING,
READING, THE ARTS -
WHATEVER BRINGS YOU PEACE

A Thought

First steps of my healing

For me, the first step in my healing was the realization that I needed to heal. Often we get so used to going through the motions of everyday life and pushing down the feelings of pains and open wounds. We are not taught to nurture our emotions but instead to ignore them because "life goes on". I allowed myself to mourn and grieve for my pain. Allowing myself to scream "It's not fair!" at the top of my lungs without judgement nor retort. Shed tears for the girl I was and all the things that made me the woman that I am. I listened to myself vent. Cried on my shoulder. And loved on the me that was hurt and encouraged her for the healing journey ahead.

"Those eyes, how mesmerizing. They sparkle, even in darkness because the shining light is not from the outside reflection but rather the inward illumination beaming from the soul."

Is It That Time?

#NowPlaying – All Alone by Dru Hill

When is it gonna be the time that my mindset changes and I stop expecting past experiences to apply to future situations?

When is it gonna be the time when I take a kiss for all it's worth instead of demeaning the value expecting ulterior motives?

When is it gonna be the time that my armored heart finally stops having it's back against the world?

Is it time to allow someone to prove themselves worthy?

Is it time that I let go of inhibitions?

Or is it just another time where loneliness manifests itself into a feeling of desire and attraction that is seemingly more intense and has a false sense of perfect timing.

Cupid, Draw Your Bow

#NowPlaying – Cupid by Sam Cooke

Grasping for imitation love.

A tangible substitute to fulfill my need for the amorous feeling without being subjected to the consequences, trials and tribulations of the real thing.
　Love.

Most desire it, and few find what it means to feel it true.

One of the most popular topics of conversation.
One of the most common causes for distraction.
One of God's most precious gifts.

Often illustrated, personified and emphasized in a positive hyperbole that I have yet to see proven.

Who's to say true love is even possible amongst mortals?

Perhaps the sins of the flesh & weakness to lust counteract and void the purity and innocence of love, therefore making it unattainable while we are still in the form of Adam and Eve.

If so, I will continue to humor imitation love and pretend the counterfeit emotions and happiness will suffice.

Today I'm grateful for:

Prayer Works

I would like to pray for:

The Rose

*#NowPlaying – The Rose That Grew from Concrete by
Tupac Shakur*

I am not a rose that grew from concrete,
but rather the rose surrounded by weeds.

They've attacked my roots which caused me to wither,
but I've not lost the power within.

God has provided me with storms so that from tears,
the water may nurture me back to health.

He has blessed me with sunshine in the most unexpected
places by people unaware of their purpose in my life.

This rose will now flourish abundantly,
defeating all that stands in the way,
so that true beauty may once again blossom.

LETTERS

Dear Childhood Amburger,

You are an amazing little person! Already showing leadership skills and interest in learning and teaching others. You have unlimited potential and can grow up to do and be anything so try it all! For all the things you try and catch on to immediately, that's amazing but remember just because you are good at something doesn't me you have to do it. Sometimes it's the things you have to study and practice that end up being the most fulfilling. There are skills you haven't discovered yet and you don't have to be a natural to participate in them.

You have been given the gift of positive communication from the adults in your family. As a child, many don't experience that so don't take it for granted! If you can share your opinion with Mommy, then you can share your opinion with your teachers. Just because they lead the classroom doesn't mean they are perfect, and they definitely don't know everything. Keep it respectful but also respect yourself. Don't let their words change who you are.

Trust your intuition! You be knowing, even at your age! If it doesn't seem or sound right, it probably isn't.

And finally, enjoy this time – it is rare, and some adults spend their lives trying to get back to the freedom and fun of childhood. Live it up!

Keep it cute,
Amb

Dear Teenage Amber - Da Next Star,

Be encouraged! I know middle school was rough and you are trying to find your way. As bad as you want to, remember, you don't have to find a place to fit in! Your vibe attracts your tribe and there are people that think and are interested in the same things you are. Once you find them, be yourself. Let your guard down. Enjoy those people! Friendships based on something real outlast the bonds based on a façade.

Also, don't let these people fool you, the main ones focused on popularity at this age end up busted and clueless after they graduate and going through an awkward stage as an adult. The grass ain't greener boo.

Can't forget, we have to talk about boys. Don't stress, believe it or not, there are quite a few cute boys that like you in secret, you'll find out later but for now don't let that be your focus. You aren't missing out on anything and the "high school sweetheart" train ain't it, trust me. Buy yourself a Valentine carnation and be your own secret admirer. Take pride in not being pressed about having a boyfriend. Go to the movies with friends. Those moments will be way more fulfilling; I promise.

Just focus on your own self-esteem and confidence. Find your passion and run towards it. The social side is better in your 20s anyway.

Peace, love and smooches
Amb

P.S – If I wasn't clear, IGNORE THAT BOY, he ain't worth it, you know the one, your intuition already told you. And so did your momma.

Dear Pregnant Amber,

Do not be ashamed, it is going to be hard but use this as a time to rethink your life and be motivated by your situation. Listen to "Zion" by Lauryn Hill. You are not alone, and you are far from the only person to have ever gone through this. Sit down with your loved ones and have an honest conversation about how you feel and what you want to do. Fear is false evidence appearing real. You have a strong support system and they can help if you let them.

It doesn't matter what anyone thinks! You have one life to live and you have to life it for yourself and your future children. Everything else is secondary. Use this situation to be a blessing to yourself and others. Reach out to other pregnant women your age, be there for one another.

Ignore the narrative of being a statistic! Black women are the statistics for everything, ignore it! You can still get everything you want in this life without settling.

Take care of yourself physically, mentally, emotionally and spiritually. Anything that doesn't find into a box that makes you happy, push it to the side. Be the woman now that you want your child to emulate. Love and forgive yourself. You are still amazing.

With love,
Amb

Dear Jade – my pumpkin pie punkin',

I've been wanting to write you again for a while. I appreciate you coming to help me. I didn't realize at the time, but you changed me. I go through life feeling like I can do anything because I survived physically losing you. I have so much empathy for others because I can understand how someone ends up in unexpected situations and feels hopeless. I understand the importance of working through our troubles and staying strong while still gifting ourselves grace. I can see how judging others is a detriment to our community. There's so much I've learned from you that I carry with me every second of everyday.

I imagine you at different ages and how you might look but then I remember the most important part of you is your spirit, that continues to walk with me.

Remember that time we were in the living room and you were standing on the couch? You walked over to me, just learning how to stand (which I now realize was extremely early given your age) and you placed your hand on my cheek. You knew I needed that comfort, and in that moment, I felt the true age of your soul. All I can express is my love and gratitude. Thank you.

Love you always,
Mommy

To Those That Need to Hear This,

You deserve better, they are not going to change, and your life is important, why play with it? No matter what your situation is, these words still apply. People are who they show you they are, believe that. Words can cause confusion, but the average person can only fake their actions for so long. It's hard when your logical mind and your emotions are at war with each other, but you have to break away from that and recognize your worth.

Also, ignore the judgment from others. This is a hard one because often the judgment comes from those, we love who's opinion we actually value. I'm sure you know those that have your best interest in mind, but sometimes the delivery isn't the best. Understand that it is hard for people to empathize for situations that they haven't experienced. And unfortunately, that can leave us on this end feeling ashamed, embarrassed and as if we have to deal with things on our own. Please put your pride aside and reach out for the help you need.

If you haven't heard it or felt it recently or ever, I love you. Even as a stranger, wherever you are, I stand with you. I wish you well and pray for your safety. Hopefully my words reach your heart.

Please be well,
Amber

Dear Younger Self,

Love,

Dear Future Self,

Love,

THANK YOU
#NowPlaying – Thank You by Boyz II Men

Lord, thank you for the strength and dedication to finish this book! I want to thank my writing coach, Bethany Loper. When I started this journey. Originally, I was looking for a ghostwriter. I wanted to feed my story to a stranger so they could regurgitate it back to all of you. Bethany not only dissuaded me from wanting to have someone else tell my story but empowered me to get it out. There have been times I've wanted to give up and she continued to speak life into me.

I want to thank and apologize to my family. I wish I could undo all the hurt and pain I've caused and chaos that I've brought into our lives but I am so grateful to have a family that, throughout my journey, have never disowned me and continued to smother me in love and support! I love y'all so much! Special shoutout to Keandra & Brittany—you two make me so proud and I thank God for the women you have become. Let my choices bring you wisdom.

To my boo boo, my love and my best friend Daiquian. I know it is not easy to love someone with so much baggage, but you are there to wipe the tears, to comfort after the nightmares and show me continuous love. To the reader, you can overcome anything! Live in your truth, know

yourself and start today by living your best version, it's never too late.

Honorable Mentions

Amanda Lovelace, you changed how I view storytelling. Andrea Morris, for being the first person to invest in my book. Chase Bell & Shannon Bond-Cover, thank you for your feedback, giving me the courage to say the book is done! Gabrielle Union, Keke Palmer, Taraji P Henson & Tiffany Haddish - for sharing your stories. To everyone that was part of my journey, short-term or long-term, you've helped to shape and create this masterpiece.

Made in the USA
Las Vegas, NV
19 March 2021